THE WONDERFUL WORLD
OF FRIENDS

The Wonderful World of Friends

Time to Make it Real

Darrell A. Roberts

authorHOUSE®

AuthorHouse™
1663 Liberty Drive
Bloomington, IN 47403
www.authorhouse.com
Phone: 1-800-839-8640

Published by AuthorHouse 6/19/2012

ISBN: 978-1-4772-1999-7 (sc)
ISBN: 978-1-4772-1998-0 (hc)
ISBN: 978-1-4772-1997-3 (e)

Library of Congress Control Number: 2012910933

Previous works by author

Pure Love Passing Through

The Long Lasting Love of Lady and Lord

THE WONDERFUL WORLD
OF FRIENDS

The above is the word "Friend"
in ancient Egyptian Hieroglyphs.

Dedication

"This book is dedicated to all who share the idea of eternal peace and pure love. You are my true friends and my loving audience. I wish you the best always."

Author's Preface

My inspiration for The Wonderful World of Friends is the spiritual world, a world where everyone is full of bliss, knowledge and life is eternal. In the spiritual world we also have mystical abilities like telepathy, teleportation etc. There is no need for mechanical technology in my vision of the spiritual world because we could make our minds desires manifest by our will. The most important thing in the spiritual world is our friendships.

I have been most fortunate to have had many people in my life who have contributed to my development. I am very grateful to these people so I wrote this book as a way to let them know that they have a place of significance in my life. The Wonderful World of Friends is a book of names in poetic form that has each name singing their own song. The goal of this book is to have a place where loved once could come live in peace and happiness.

<u>Acknowledgment</u>

All praise and glories be to God!! I would like to acknowledge my friends and family always. Their love and support have brought me through some dark times, I will always do my best to honor you all.

Contents

<u>Introduction</u>

In life there are many choices a person must make to help them secure the outcome that is desired, and that desire is to be happy. Considering all the choices that a person must make, association is one of the most important choices in the life of a person. Once a person is fully conscious of this fact, a determined person will have the ability to improve on their life's circumstance. This may seem like a very simple idea; however, looking at my own life and the lives of those around me, I know it is easier said than done.

The <u>Wild and Wonderful World of Friends</u> is a book that focuses on this idea that our choices in friends will influence who we will become. I chose the title of this book because in my eyes this world is wild and chaotic, yet it is still wonderful because there are so many outstanding people whom I have encountered. I consider these people special and irreplaceable in the world that we share.

The goal of this particular book is to immortalize my friends by writing an ode to hold their memory eternally. It is while we are here together, in this life, we could say what we desire to say to each other, therefore, I have chosen to profess my sincerely love for certain people while I am still here, since tomorrow is not a guarantee.

There is a belief amongst some of us that souls travel through time and space together for eternity. If you ever have gotten the feeling when you meet a stranger, but it seems like you have always known them your whole life you could relate to what I mean. Have you ever had dreams that seemed so real where your friends and family are there time after time? Perhaps you go to call a friend and as you pick up the phone it rings and they are on the other line.

The Wonderful World of Friends is written for people who appreciate true loving relationships and are willing to go the distance, through time and space for eternity with loved ones. The book is to inspire those who see this world as a world that could use much improving, by reminding them that this is the temporary world all we can do is the best we can here and with faith and determination we will find better in the next world(s) until we all make it back home to the spiritual world.

I sincerely hope that anyone who picks up the Wonderful World of Friends enjoys the reading and works toward creating their own wonderful world here and now as well as there and then.

Going back home

Time to take a look and do what is right
Find the strength to let go of this world here
This world is full of dangers day and night
Time to go back home where there is no fear
This world is temporary my good friend
Back home we live life in eternal bliss
This world makes it hard to tell what's pretend
In this world it is peace that I do miss
The soul heart and mind must be free in life
When we are home we all share the same song
When we are home there is peace and not strife
Back home we play sing and laugh all day long
We will need nothing once we return home
Our fantastic father will give all
We will have all knowledge of self there known
We should return to the Lord's Loving call.
For: All Peaceful Loving Beings
By: Darrell A. Roberts

Our World

Our world and love is real, this is how we feel
Together we are Devine, with souls intertwined
Here trying to build a dream, together a team
Together with all our friends, until this sweet world ends
The pure love we have will hold, it will not grow old
We will sing our sweet song, proudly all day and night long
Our hearts will merge as one, here under the sun
In the night time we are a star. We really know who we are
We will walk strong ere through time, as we live life's rhyme
No matter what we will do, my love know that I love you

Alvin

Always there on Time to stand with a friend
Living Life providing Hope to all here
Vibrant and brilliant he will not bend
In this life He is fervent with no fear
Needless to say that His will sets the trend
Silently He stands strong and lends and ear

Always awesome He lives like a Lion
Lover of Life He strives to stop all strife
Victorious He comes a champion
In His long lasting story He serves Life
Needless to say He's a nice companion
Sharing His wits that are sharp like a knife

Always He will stand tall he is a wall
Letting no one pass unless they are true
Victory vibrates when ever He call
In this world he tries his best to come through
Needless to say that the this friend will not fall
Silently He will stand strong just for You.

<u>Andre</u>

Awesomely He stands strong playing the drum
No One can touch Him He is Great MAHA*
Dark and daring please not he's not a bum
Ready to release His super kind KA*
Each stroke he strikes is a thump not a hum

Always He is there fighting for His Friend
No One can challenge His awesome power
Do not think that you can make His will bend
Remember He does not cringe or cower
Everyone knows He will win in the End

Always He works for others happiness
No One can dare say that He is not true
Daringly He Helps Others in distress
Readily He is there to pull them through
Each time he is there to Help clean the mess

Andre' my good man you're one of the best
No One can deny your goodness of heart
Displaying true knowledge from east to west
Ready to present your Soul's perfect part?
Each step of the way will be a true test!!!

Andrea

An awesome spirit who shines like a star
No one will ever stop her from shining
Doing her best work she will travel far
Readily she will be there just smiling
Each day she will make strides to raise the bar

Adorable with sweet enchanting eyes
Needless to say she has a real warm heart
Delivering the truth she don't tell lies
Ready like a leader to do her part
Each day her sweet song will brighten the skies
Always her sweet words will sound like true art

Another bright star in this world right here
No one will deny that her fire is hot
Doing her best to fight off any fear
Ready to rule her world she will not stop
Each one that meets her will see how she care
Always she will triumph and stay on top

<u>Andrew</u>

Always there protecting a favored friend
Never does He let any harm touch them
Daringly He moves firth and sets the trend
Ready to show His glow just like a gem
Ever perfect and real He won't pretend
We will wonder from where His wisdom stem

Always He knows what's the best thing to say
No One can stop His song from singing here
Daringly He takes charge and leads the way
Ready to guide His true Friends with no fear
Ever inspiring to all each day
We will stand in Awe when ever He's near

Always I see Him as an ancient King
No One can test Him because He'll win
Daringly he will stand strong as He sing
Ready to be kind he is human's kin
Ever He will be there loyal and loving
Who would den His greatness commits sin!!

<u>Angels</u>

An Awesome being that protects all Love
Never will they fail and let you fall
Giving gratitude to the One above
Every time they are there just for your call
Living among us they soar like a dove
Showing us how to overcome the wall

Angels awaken and know who you are
Never let others think that you aren't real
Give them the light like a sweet shining star
Empower their day just like the real deal
Live here happy with US and lead US far
Such a great grand being don't conceal

Angels are the great guides for the living
Needless to say they they're thoughtful souls here
Giving US all Hope while sweetly singing
Ever enchanting they are with no fear
Living the strong style of Life when fighting
Showing US the correct way 'cause they care!!!!

Annand

An awesome shining star in this world here
No one will stop him from doing his best
Now he lives his life in Love and not fear
Always he will win in this life's great test
Now he speaks from the heart yes he does care
Doing his best he'll come through east to west

All will see him as a generous king
No one will deny his friendship or fame
Now he lives life just to do the right thing
Always he will win in life that's the aim
Now it is special heart that will sing
Doing his best he will win this great game

Always he will shine in life as a star
No one will ever block his loving light
Now his light will shine so very far
Another brother who will shine so bright
Now he is the one that will raise the bar
Doing his best to bring wrong things to right

Annie

An awesome Lady's is she and a Friend
Now if you test her heart know she will win
No one can say such goodness is pretend
In her heart she strives not to commit sin
Each day her good work will set the good trend

Always she is sweet thoughtful peaceful and kind
No one can call her any unkind name
Now we will see her great mystical mind
It is building a brighter world's her aim
Each one will see she's a terrific find

An out standing person we will watch shine
Needless to say that she has a good heart
No one can challenge her love is divine
It is such art watching her play her part
Each day she will age like an awesome wine

Always an eagle she watches life's show
Not like a snake she will soar high in life
No one will stop her pure heart she ill flow
It is her strength that will stop Life's strife
Ever her great spirit will seek to grow.

Antarami

An awesome person with such a kind heart
No one can dispute that he is divine
This magnificent man is living art
Always he shines like a star in this line
Radiating such great care and such charm
A great and generous soul in this life
Mighty is his mind his heart is so warm
It is he who will help others in Strife

Always he will be a true champion
No one will ever stop his shining star
This terrific man is one of action
Always he will win the internal war
Radiant he shines through any gray sky
A powerful pillar he stands so strong
Making the right moves so that he will fly high
It is his goodness and love that last long

<u>Anvor</u>

Awesome among all the Angels he shines
No one can challenge his goodness of heart
Victorious are all his loving lines
Opener of eyes he share his great art
Readily he stands strong he never whines

Always he will teach and train his good man
Never will he back down nor will he fail
Victory in this life is the true plan
Over all challenges his soul will sail!
Ready to show the whole world what he can

A super shining star his soul is Free
No one can ever bind This pure sweet soul
Victory is his song we all will see
Only pure perfect Love is his goal
Readily he stand strong just like a tree

Always he seeks out his kind favored friends
No one can challenge his goodness of heart
Very loyal and loving the words he sends
Opening the world's eyes with awesome art
Ready to win until this world ends!
By Darrell Roberts

Bushara

Brilliantly he shines a beacon of light
Having the heart to hear Lord Krsna's call
Upright he uplifts the souls of us all
Sharing his love he's a light that shines bright
An awesome being who does what is right
Readily he prevents friends from a fall
Always awesome he is not here to fight

Bringing spiritual bliss where he go
He provides pleasure in life and not strife
Upright Krsna's kind devotee this life
Shining as a star in Lord Krsna's show
An angel sent here to help others grow
Ready to live with love not with the knife
An awesome one who helps those who fell low

Beautiful is his sweet smile for the friend
Having the strength to give Krsna glory
Upright his loving laugh tells the story
Strong lie a statue he does not pretend
An awesome devotee whose will won't bend
Read to reveal the allegory
A gentle and great being 'till the end.

Brian

Bringing forth beautiful thoughts from his heart
Readily He stands strong for what is right
In this day and Time he will stand apart
Awesomely displaying his mental might
No one will deny His world of His art

Brainy he may be his true love is (real) pure
Readily He will help through out all Time
In this short story His friendships the (deal) cure
Always He will be here ready to Rhyme
No one can say his goodness is impure

Besting His rivals He will lead the way
Running toward His great goal He sets the stage
In this Life's drama He stars in the play
Always awake with wisdom in this age
No One may test His heat that's what I say

Brian is a bright light and a true Friend
Readily He takes cars of those He love
In this day and Time this truth does not bend
Always inspired by Great God above
Needless to say He'll be there in the End.

Bruce

Brilliantly he shines a true super star
Readily guiding others to the Real
Understanding who we all really are
Caring to consider how we will feel
Enchantingly he helps them raise the bar

Bringing the Lord's loving light to the Friend
Readily he sings sweetly every day
Under the smiling sun he don't pretend
Calmly and carefully he leads the way
Enchanting each one he meets 'till the end

Brightening this wonderful world with song
Readily he helps the minds of many
Until the very end he will stand strong
Carefully he fixes flaws if any
Each one should know that his love will last long

Building beautiful bonds with devotees
Readily he shares his great light with all
Understand he stands strong just like the trees
Carefully he calls all before they fall
Ever does his love flow like the Lord's seas!

Carrington

Caring to provide and protect true love
An Awesome brother who is a bright star
Radiant like the sun he shines high above
Ready to travel through time very far
In this short story he soars like dove
No one can stop him he will win his war
Gently he will guide us he will not shove
Taking his time to find out who we are
Opening the master's door for true love
No one can deny on land he stands par

Carefully championing his great art
An awesome King he roars like a lion
Ready to protect the pride is his part
Ready is this mighty man of action
In this mighty man lives such a great heart
No one can challenge this true champion
Greatly he helps others with their great start
This star shines and strives for perfection
Opening his mighty mind to great art
No one can dispute his dedication

Charlie

Carefully he guides us all around town
Having the heart of a lion he's strong
Always shining on all white black or brown
Ready to speak what is right not what's wrong
Look how his face smiles and it will not frown
In him will sing the kindest sweetest song
Ever he lives like a king with no crown

Caring to make this world a better place
Having the Lion's courage he is brave
Always he has such a calm handsome face
Ready to feed knowledge to those who crave
Like royalty he walks with great grand grace
It is he who will live well 'till the grave
Excellently he moves through with no trace

Calmly he greets and takes care of the guest
Here he plays the perfect role of a Friend
Always there attentive he is the best
Ready to provide the rules he won't bend
Like a great student he will pass life's test
It is he who will sing well in the End
Each soul will respect him from east to west

Chatamayi

Charming and caring s this great Lady
Having the heart to love every person
Always she plays her music so sweetly
This Lovely lady's heart's warm like the sun
A rose in this world that's bloomed perfectly
Many may find her a great champion
Always she soars high in the sky freely
You will find of her kind there is just one
In this life she guides others gently

Calmly she chants to the great God Visnu
Her heart focusing on the mystical sound
Always for her true friends she will come through
Taking the time to know friends that she's found
Always she will be beloved by the crew
Making music for Krsna all around
Anyone can see that it's for heaven she's bound
Yes she shares her sweet music all around
In this world like her there are very few.

Chienhwe (1000 Virtues)

Champion of Children the lady stands strong
Having a happy heart and awesome smile
I see in her a great Taiwanese song
Encouraging is her excellent style
No one can ever say she is not kind
Her pure and true virtues radiates like Sun
When you see her eyes they will sooth your mind
Ever special she will be until time's done

Charming is she with a sweet vibrant voice
Her great compassion shines through her heart
If you see her sweet smile you will rejoice
Embracing the goodness in this great life
No one can challenge her sweet loving heart
With her Yoga she will stop life's great strife
Every motion she makes is like pure art

Crystal

Careful is this lovely lady to me
Radiantly she shines she glows she flows
Yes she has great depth like the clear blue sea
She move through life with great grace as she goes
Talented and tough is this great lady
A lotus flower watch how she will grow
Like a strong tree she stands just look and see

Charming is her smile and enchanting eyes
Radiant like Sun she brightens the way
Yes you can tell that she is very wise
She shines so bright just like a solar ray
This lovely lady the truth not lies
Always she will sing her great song each day
Let a true friendship with her be the prize

Cheerful is the room when lady is there
Readily she shows a good woman
Yes she lives life with courage not fear
Strong lioness she shows that she can
This shining star will brighten a anywhere
A lady who could help better her man
Like a great goddess she'll do as she dare

Dallas

Doing her best she shares her heart with all
A lovely Lady and a great Goddess
Living with Love in her heart she won't fall
Like bright stars at night she shines happiness
Always cool and calm when ever she call
She shares her hope and removes the distress

Doing her best to live life free from fear
A Quiet Queen who stands strong all day long
Like a warm comforter she shows great care
Like the stars shining she will sing her song
Always awesome is she when she appear
She readily does what is right not wrong

Doing her best she will sing her great rhyme
A picture perfect princess she is kind
Look at how she will shine through life in time
Loving her favored friends she's a great find
Always truthful she does not commit crime
She has a great heart and a mighty mind

Daniel

Daring to take the lead He is the man
Awesomely He calculates like a clock
Nothing in this whole world will stop The plan
It is in him to conquer the road block
Everyone knows he's the head of the clan
Love in his heart like a clock beats tick tock

Doing His best to pass this life's tough test
Always awesomely giving to the All
Nothing will slow him down from east to west
It is the good class that will hear his call
Each bright one here he will bring out their best
Leading them in life to rise not to fall

Daniel The one who lets God be the judge
An angelic person and a true friend
No way he could ever hold a hard grudge
In this life his will to Love will not bend
Ever he is like a bear he won't budge
Letting his sweet star sine until the end.

Dasarath

Dong the best he can to live in Love
An awesome shining star he is so bright
Soaring like an eagle he'll rise above
Always his light will shine right through the night
Ready to lead the way he's a good man
Always taking his time to do things right
This valiant Vaisnava has a great plan
He inspires others with his great insight

Doing the best he can he's a great dad
Always trying to guide his children well
Staying peaceful and sane he won't get mad
Always he will live free not in a cell
Ready to uplift friends that are sad
Always with compassion for souls who fell
This brilliant devotee is not bad
He is a true and pure friend to Darrell

Debbie

Doing the best that she can in this life
Each day she strives to remain positive
Building beautiful bonds not causing strife
Blessing those who pass by that's how she live
It's lasting love she has it's not the knife
Each thought that she has is not negative

Doing her best she will always shine strong
Each tough circumstance will challenge her heart
Brilliantly she will shine day and night long
Bringing forth her hearts inner world as art
It is her words that will be right not wrong
Each step that she takes perfect from the start

Doing her true best to do what is right
Each moment here she helps others each day
Bringing forth the goodness of her mind's might
Being a leader here showing the way
It is her duty for goodness to fight
Ever a shining star in the Lord's play

By: Darrell A. Roberts

__Devon__

Doing the best he can despite Life's Strife
Each day a challenge that he must fight through
Victory is his through love not the knife
Openly he shows he loves the crew
No one must trouble this one in this Life

Doing his best this little star will shine
Each day he will stand strong and sing his song
Victory is his for he is divine
Openly he does what is right not wrong
No one to him should speak an unkind line

Dear is this person to the on who writes
Each day moves us toward the great destiny
Victory will choose us through out all the fights
Openly we will show what's sanity
No one will say we don't shine as bright lights

Dare I say we have stood strong from the start
Each day brings us new fights from the mind
Victory we will play the good part
Openly we will both show that we're kind
No one will say our work is not art

By: Darrell A. Roberts

<u>Dionne</u>

Daring and dashing is this great dark one
It is her strength that will always shine through
Outstanding is her Love pure like the sun
No one can deny she toughens the crew
Never will she quit until the work is done
Each day she takes the lead one of the few

Doing her best is Lady Lioness
In this wonderful world she makes the day bright
Overcoming this world's life and its stress
No one can lessen Lady's loving light
Needless to say Lady does not depress
Each day she manifests her minds great might

Daily she shines like a great super star
Insider her is true compassion and care
Openly she'll help favored friends move far
No one can say that she lives life with fear
Never will she live her life in a bar
Each day it is her goodness that she will share

<u>Dolores</u>

Doing her best to shine throughout all time
Opening the door so others may win
Lovely is this lady in this life's Rhyme
Opening her mind you'll find her like kin
Readily she helps and commits no crime
Ever willing to see beyond the skin
She will shine bright until the last chime

Doing wonderful works to help the young star
Opening her heart showing how she cares
Like a spaceship she sure will go far
Opening her mind she'll live free from fear
Ready to roll through this world like a car
Everyday she live life as she dares
Showing the world it's time to raise the bar

Doing her best as the child's Champion
Opening their eyes to a greater life
Like a great athlete she takes strong action
Openly she takes a stand to stop strife
Ready to share and give satisfaction
Ever she will be a wonderful wife
She will live life free and well in fashion

Donna

Doing her best to shine she is Devine
Opening the door to a better life
Now she will share her sweet kind loving line
Now in this life she puts an end to strife
Always with words so sweet just like fine wine

Doing her best she will always shine bright
Opening the light for all future time
Now all will see her love and mental might
Now she will radiate such a great rhyme
Always she will live with love in the light

Doing her best she has great charm and grace
Opening her heart she is really kind
Now she shines like the sun with a sweet face
Now in this world she's a wonderful find
Always she will help out the human race

Doing her best to live life without fears
Opening her mighty mind to the Friend
Now she will take time to show that she cares
Now she stands strong for each friend 'till the end
Always she will have two excellent ears

Doreatha

Daringly with love she will lead the way
Opening the minds of others each day
Ready to live in peace is what she pray
Each person should listen to what she'll say
Always there for a friend with out delay
This woman shines just like a solar ray
Her heart is warm and friendly never gray
Always standing strong difficult to sway

Daringly like a star she is shining
Opening the door for all who's winning
Ready with love right from the beginning
Each person will see her brilliance beaming
Always with kindness her work is binding
Taking the time to talk when out dining
Having determination when working
Always an awesome woman when standing

Doing her best for the true favored Friend
Opening her mighty mind she'll defend
Ready through out the world her love she'll send
Ever pure in truth she does not pretend
Always finding flaws to fix patch or mend
This woman is who will start the new trend
Here the lovely lioness does not bend
Always she will shine bright until the END

<u>Doug</u>

During the day he shines bright like the sun
Opening his heart and his mind to all
Unlike others he fights he does not run
Gaining his great glory he will not fall

Daringly he tries to defend the weak
Only sometime he may just be too bold
Upright his world is bright it is not bleak
Granted his smile keeps him from getting old

Doing the best he can to be the man
Opening his mighty mind for great change
Unlike others he will perfect his plan
Getting to the source no matter how strange

Dominating the way that his mind thinks
Only he can find his true soul's freedom
Upright his love will be sweet not stink
Giving goodness until Dark Death will come

Drusilla

Doing her best to share her lasting love
Readily like a bird she soars high above
Under the great grand sky pure like a dove
She will be known by the sweet name Belove
In this wonderful world she will shine bright
Like the stars at night she will show her might
Living life well she will do what is right
Always striving for peace and not to fight

Doing her best to care and comfort all
Ready to catch her friends before they fall
Under the bright blue sky she sees no wall
Standing strong singing with a loving call
In this wonderful woman's a great heart
Leading the way perfect she plays her part
Living her awesome life a work of art
Always her sound is sweet it is not tart

Doing her best she opens her mighty mind
Ready to carefully chant you will find
Under the night time sky stars she will bind
She shines so brightly because she is kind
In any ancient time she is a friend
Look at how thoughtfully her love she send
Living with pure love she does not pretend
Always she will stand strong until the end.

Durwin

Daringly he tries to do what is right
Under heavens canopy he does care
Readily for a true friend her will fight
Walking through this world with strength as he dares
In this strong story he's a man of might
No one can stop his will he has no fear

Daringly he faces forces all day
Under the clouds is mighty mind still shines
Readily is he to find the best way
Working well with brothers we play and dine
In this perfect play he won't run away
Now listen as he lets loose the great line

Daringly his soul will sing sweet song
Under the shining stars he still is real
Readily in this world he will stand strong
Walking with his bright light that is the deal
In this sweet story he does not do wrong
Now he's a favored friend that's how we feel

Ella

Enchanting the Earth with her pleasant smiles
Living life well she has a humble heart
Look at how she has ran so many miles
Awesomely she shines as she plays her part

Ever she shines brightly a super star
Letting no one dim or darken her light
Look at how she lives she will travel far
Always displaying her might she shines bright

Ever sweet like a rose she smells the best
Look at how she plays with such pure love
Look at how she transcends right through life's test
Always singing her song from high above

Enhancing the lives of her favored friends
Letting her cherished ones know that she cares
Look she will stay strong until this time ends
Always she will conquer her deep dark fears

Elliot

Excellently he Builds Bonds that will last
Long after we are gone his mark will stand
Leading like the Pharaoh of ancient past
It is his will that will restore the land
Opening his mighty mind that runs fast
This mighty man takes great care of his band

Excellently he views life with his eyes
Look how he shines as a true Sun of Light
Living like the good sun under God's Skies
It is his purity that is his might
Opening his heart he will win the prize
This man does his best to do what is right

Excellently he guides those in the dark
Living with true Love he serves as a Friend
Like a Lord Lion he roars so now hark
In him lives lasting love he don't pretend
Opening his soul he shares his great spark
This mighty man will last until the End

__Emily__

Excellent are her kind enchanting eyes
Magically she moves lie a true queen
In this world she shine under the skies
Lovely is her laugh in every scene
You will see that this Lady's truly wise

Enriching the lives of all those she meets
Magnificently is show she lives life
Inspiring Friends with all her great feats
Living life with Love over coming strife
Yes she is gentle to all who she greets

Enchanting the class she shows that she cares
Making life brighter and better for all
In this wild world she lives free from fears
Looking out for the Friend before they fall
Yes she has courage and does as she dares

Ever open minded she thinks things through
Mentally stable she's like a statue
In this wild world helping that's what she'll do
Living life happily one of the few
Yes her good human heart is pure and true

<u>Eric</u>

Excellent eyes lets Him enchant the class
Readily He radiates his wisdom
In school his knowledge is gold, not like brass
Carefully He counsels all as they come
Each one that meets him He gives them His best
Readily He stands strong for the student
Instructing them how to conquer Life's test
Carefully teaching them of management
Each one that sees Him shine will know he's great
Readily He directs those who will hear
In this world He teaches on time not late
Carefully He calls for us while we're here
Encouraging others to open eyes,
Readily He teaches them to finance
In class He makes things clear like blue skies
Carefully He teaches the numbers Dance.

Gail

Great is her gentle smile her care and charm,
Always she finds a way to show her love,
In this world her wonderful heart is warm,
Like the free falcon she will fly above.

Giving is her nature she is so kind,
Always she will triumph through this life's test,
I know that she is a true friend to find,
Like the sun her rays shine from east to west.

Gentle is her mighty mind in this life,
Always awesome she will bring joy to all
In this wild world she will fight through life's strife
Like the lioness she will never fall

Great is her sweet spirit that she will share
Always with shining eyes she sings her song
In this enchanting earth she conquers fear,
Like the tall tree she'll stand strong all life long.

Garvin

Greatly honored are those who will see him
Always an awesome majestic vision
Ready to save this wild world on a whim
Victorious he shines in each season
In his perfect plan he moves with rhythm
No one can harm him for any reason

Giving generously he is a king
Awesome with mental might he's out o sight
Ready in his heart with good tunes to sing
Victoriously his star will shine bright
In this story it's the light he will bring
Now he tries hard to do what is right

Giving the world a great smile and true joy
Always a brother no matter how far
Ready to be up front and not coy
Victoriously he is a super star
In this wonderful world he's a big boy
Now he will do his best to raise the bar

Gloria

Gloriously she graces every place
Letting others see that she will shine here
Openly she wears a smile on her face
Readily she could run miles anywhere
In this day and time she walks with great grace
Always living life with Love and not fear

Glowing brightly in the baddest of nights
Letting her sweet soul find love and shine through
Openly she stands one of the bright lights
Readily she shares kindness that is true
In this Rhyme she stands and fights for her rights
Always a running friend that's what we do

Glowing brightly she's a great shining star
Lovingly she cares for children in life
Openly telling them how great they are
Readily in this life she will stop strife
In this world a being who'll raise the bar
Always living with Love not with the knife

<u>Horace</u>

Here in this day and time He is the Man
Only He can stand to the mighty one
Radiating He shines like a star can
Always doing work until The Jobs Done
Carefully He protects The Devine plan

Here having Hope is how he Lives His life
Only Providing Help he is a friend
Readily He would stop all of Life's Strife
Always He tells the real He don't pretend
Carefully He calls His children and wife
Everyone knows He'll be there in the End.

Here I watch Him and I see a young star
Only time will tell if He shines His light
Readily for this friend I will travel far
Always we may call on His might
Carefully He'll challenge and raise the bar,
Each time we see His eyes we'll see His light

Ibrahym

It is he who will come to save the day
Bringing his Friendship and his loving light
Radiating like Sun in The Lord's play
Awesomely he displays his mental might
Having courage he chases villains away
Yes He is a Super Star that shines Bright
Making other stars shine without delay

In him lives the heart of a true kind king
Bringing forth goodness to brighten the day
Ready to assist all he is thinking
Always willing to share he shows the way
Having Hope and courage always helping
Yes he lives as a leader in this play
Making magic happen not just praying

It is a great smile his spirit will send
Boldly he takes a strong stand in this land
Ready to defend those that he calls Friend
Always awesomely by Friends he will stand
Having a true heart he does not pretend
Yes he will stand strong until we disband
Mightily his star will shine 'till the END!!

<u>Irene</u>

In this wonderful world sweet is her smile
Readily she triumphs through life's great test
Each moment she shines with great style
Now she stands strong as one of this world's best
Each day ready to run more than a mile

In our pure perfect play she is kind
Ready to run the world she has no fear
Each one that meets her thinks she's a good friend
No one can defeat her they do not dare
Each thought that she has is cleansed by her mind

In her is a wonderful woman here
Ready to give care and comfort to all
Each day she lives life with love not the knife
Now she is a true caring friend to call
Ever her star will shine bright every where

In her life radiant rhyme she will win
Ready to let her love flow like the sea
Each day she strives not to commit sin
Now what a wonderful woman we'll see
Each kind soul she meets feel like she is kin!!!

Jason

Just Like a star he stands the man
Always gracious gentle peaceful and kind
Showing the world what makes a great human
Only a true perfect prince you will find
No one will challenge his wonderful plan

Just like a bright star he will shine through time
Always wonderful and warm is his heart
Sharing his sweet song and his great Life's rhyme
Open his door and you will see great art
No way will this good man commit crime

Just like the Lion he'll move like a king
Always seeking ways to shine in this life
Sharing the great song that his heart will sing
Overcoming any of this life's strife
Now see the good to this world he will bring

Just like an Eagle we will watch him soar
Always he will assist all his good friends
Showing his strength like a lion he'll roar
Original one he'll set all the trends
Now he's a man of peace not one of war

Jessica

Just a Joy to be around this princess
Ever so pleasant this enchanting one
She will be the one to shine through Darkness
Singing her sweet song and having great fun
In this world we will see her great brightness
Calmly she will pass through until time's done
Always she will come with her correctness

Just a wonderful person to be around
Each moment she moves with such grace and charm
She shines like a bright star that I've found
Sharing her good heart she's gentle and warm
In this wonderful world Goodness she's bound
Carefully she chooses not to do harm
Always she will remain strong above ground

Just a jubilant kind happy person
Ever hopeful she stands strong like a stone
She will overcome this world's life lesson
She sings the best song in the sweetest tone
In her will live the pure light of the sun
Champion in life she does not cry or moan
Always she will work our to be the one

Joanne

Just a beautiful person bright like a Star
Opening her mind to tell what is true
Angelic soul who will travel so far
No one will dim her light it will shine through
Now in this world here favored friends we are
Each moment doing the best we can do

Just a wonderful woman in this place
Opening her heart to help out others
Always with her friendly wonderful face
Needless to say she takes care of mothers
Needless to say she is an awesome ace
Enchanting all her sisters and brothers

Just a special person is who I see
Opening her thoughtful and mighty mind
Awesome is how she stand and show she'll be
Now she is truly one of a great kind
No one can deny that she's great to me
Each soul will know she is a great find

John

Just in his actions he is fair and kind
Opening his great heart to share with all
He is one of the greatest friends you can find
Never will he stand by and watch you fall

Jubilantly he lives life as the man
Opening his mighty mind he will win
Having hope for all is part of his plan
Never will he help on to commit sin

Jumping for joy because life is so great
Opening his great soul he is like a king
Having true courage he has more than faith
Now it is His time to stand up and sing

Joyfully cheering with care for his love
Opening his trust for the favored friend
Having the super strength to rise above
Never will this man quit until the end.

__Katrina__

Keeping the true count with her vibrant voice
Attracting kind friends with such a sweet soul
This lovely lady is an awesome choice
Radiantly she shines love is her goal
In the dojo with friends she is a star
Nothing out of her reach nothings too far
A great angel of peace not one of war

Keeping all her friends safe she is so kind
Always moving through gently with such grace
This lovely lady is a precious find
Remember her sweet smile and charming face
In my eyes she's a sweet sister to me
No one ever can say she's not friendly
A tough and thoughtful person you will see

Keeping all of her true friends in mind
Always with a pleasant smile she greets us
This lovely lady helps the mind unwind
Really she's nice to speak with we don't fuss
In the Wonderful World of All my friends
No one can say that she pretends
Always she will be friends until time ends

Kazuma

Keeping the mystical Law in his heart
Always awesomely enchanting this one
Zipping around the world playing his part
Making others see his life as great art
Always he will win until time is done

Kindly he reveals a true mighty mind
Always he will work with love in his soul
Zapping away the strife that he may find
Using the Law to fulfill his grand goal
Making the moves that will show that he's kind
Always he will be bright not dark like coal

Keeping true to the faith to bring world peace
Always he will be a true favored friend
Zipping around this world his love won't cease
Using the law with Faith his will won't bend
Making the moves to find eternal peace
Always a shining stat until the End.

Keshni

Kindness personified in my sweet song
Each Time that she smiles She brightens my day
Sweetly she sings in her heart all day long
Her sweet vibrant voice will lead the good way
No one can deny that her heart is strong
In this Rhyme and Time that's what I say

Keeping herself stabilized in this life
Each person she meets she touches their heart
She sweetly comforts them removing strife
Having the heart she plays her loving part
Now I can see that she will be the wife
In this day and Time her true love is art

Krsna and Radha's Princess Pujari
Each thought that she has is with Deity
Sharing her wisdom so others may see
Her great gentle heart is so good to me
Needless to say to my heart she holds the key
In this life here I hopes that we will be.

<u>Kevin</u>

King who will be sure to give out the Law
Each one he meets he enchants with his smile
Victorious he will be free from flaw
It is his way to travel with great style
Now he is firm in Faith not weak like straw

Kind is he to each person that he meets
Each one will greet him like a gentleman
Very awesomely accomplishing feats
In him lives the great Light's pure perfect plan
Now he knows the beautiful rhythmic beats

Keeping eyes and ears open he sees all
Each sweet soul will see him as a champion
Victorious will be his great calm call
In this wonderful world he's salvation
Now he tries to catch Friends before they fall

Keeper of the bright light inside his heart
Each one that finds him will call him a friend
Victoriously he will play his part
It is his love that will last 'till the End
Now he's a real winner right from the start

Kush

Kin like and kind is this gentleman
Upright he stands strong a true champion
Striving to deserve in sweet Lord Krsna's plan
He moves like a king this human Lion,

Kingly he has trained his mighty mind
Using his great gifts he shines as a star
Showing the whole world he is a great find
He will thoroughly travel very far

Keep his face calm with his sunshine smile
Upright the helps other to do their best
Sharing his wisdom and his unique style
He will transcend this world passing life's best

Kindly he speaks with a soft gentle voice
Using wonderful words when he's with friends
Star like he is a reason to rejoice
He will stand strong up until this world Ends

Lala

Look a Nubian Queen she is a star
Always moving sweetly throughout time
Like a cheater she will run fast and far
An awesome Lady she'll shine in this rhyme

Look how she smile with brown enchanting eyes
Absolutely beautiful is her sweet smile
Lovely is her form I tell you no lies
Always she moves with grace and such sweet style

Listen to her voice she speaks word that's kind
Always her sweet sounds vibrate with such care
Lovely is this lady a perfect find
Always she lives life with courage not fear

Lovely is this lady who leads the way
Always the good children will she her shine
Like the Sun this lady brightens the day
Always this great Goddess will shine Devine

Leila

Like a sweet loving star she leads the way
Energizing each Friend with her great deeds
Instantly there caring for different creeds
Like the shining Sun she brightens the Day
Always she laughs with such love when at play.

Leila is the key to this great man's past
Using her strength she established his faith
Causing him to see only the soul last
Always on Time to assist never late
She is a special member of my cast

Like a bright beacon she gives others hope
Enhancing others lives with her wisdom
Inside her heart there live God's Great Kingdom
Leila' Love will pull you through like a rope
Always finding a way so all my cope

Leila leads the way by good example
Using her mighty mind she makes things clear
Carefully choosing her word's a sample
Awesomely she lives her life with no fear
Showing sweet love of which she has ample

Luana

Lovingly her sweet smile gives light
Using her charm she enchants all
A heart of gold and a soul that is bright
No way she will ever let a friend fall
Awesomely she brightens the day or night

Lovingly she takes the time to help out
Using her mighty mind she leads the way
Always doing her best there is no doubt
Now she is the shining star in the day
Always she has a smile she does not pout

Lovingly she tries to do her best
Using intuition to do things right
Always triumphing over life's great test
No one will defeat her due to her might
Always she will stand strong from east to west

Lovingly helping the homeless find hope
Unsurpassed in her heart here to be kind
Assisting others to find skills to cope
Note that this woman's a wonderful find
Always a helpful hand filled with great Hope!!

Lutrecia

Lovely is she with her bright sunshine smile
Under God's great grand sky she is a Queen
Taking her time she show such a great style
Radiating like a star in each scene
Each one that meets her will know she loves life
Carefully she will call out to the friend
In this wonderful world she will stop strife
Awesomely she will shine until the end

Lovely is her soul; she's special through time
Under the beautiful sky she will glow
This shining star will create her own rhyme
Radiantly she lives life so we know
Each one that sees her will see her greatness
Calmly she will sing her sweet song to all
In this life here she will have happiness
Always she will be there so friends won't fall

<u>Marilynn</u>

Magically mystifying she shines through
Awesomely annihilating the dark
Ready to assist a Friend pure and true
In this story her sweet soul does not park
Look at how she took her time and grew
Yes she shines like a star with a great spark
No one can stop her she's one of the crew
Now is her time here to share so please hark

Making sweet music she is enchanting
Awesomely she lives life with her sweet smile
Really her energy is enhancing
In this wonderful world she has a great style
Look at the care she puts in to chanting
Yes she will win until the final mile
No one will distract her she keeps wining
Now is her time to triumph through life's trials

Marla

Making the world smile with her care and charm
Always ready to assist the good man
Readily she shares a heart that is truly warm
Loving with the man she works the plan
Always assisting she never does harm

Making her lovely light shine all so bright
Always she shines on others like the Sun
Readily she'll display her mental might
Lovingly she will shine until time's done
Always she's there to help she does not fight

Moving gracefully she looks out for all
Always thinking kind thoughts an awesome Queen
Readily she stops friends before they fall
Living with her King they will build their dream
Always to favored friends she'll place the call

Making the most of life she is happy
Always a joy to see her and talk
Readily she shines so that all may see
Living her life here the talk meets the walk
Always a beautiful star she will be

<u>Marsha</u>

Making this world much brighter by her smiles
Awesome are her enchanting eyes in life
Ready is she to display her sweet styles
She will shine like the sun straight through life's strife
Here in this life she'll travel many miles
Always living in love not with the knife

Many will see her shine like a bright star
Awesomely her rays will dispel the dark
Readily for friends she will travel far
She will win in life she won't miss the mark
Here we live at perfect peace not at war
Always she has a loving heart so hark!

Moving with good grace and charm she is kind
Awesomely she's a champion that cares
Readily she shines a diamond you'll find
She will face her challenges and fears
Here she will have bright stars that she will bind
Always she will travel through as she dares.

Michael

Many will both love and fear this great man
It is his mighty mind that wins the day
Carefully he will execute his plan
Awesome like Zeus this man proves that he can
Each day he will catch those who go astray
Like the great gods of old he stands the man

Mystical are his cool enchanting eyes
In him is a clear mind you will find
Calling what he sees this man speaks no lies
He has the heart to protect all his kind
An awesome angel we'll see how he flies
Each one that meets him will see a great mind
Lover of children he hears those who cries

Many likes when this great man takes the lead
In his students you'll see the great man's heart
Careful and courageous their story will read
He makes sure each person plays their part
A shining star he will always succeed
Each one will see the Headmaster's true art
Like a thoroughbred the man's a great steed

Michelle

Magically she moves singing her song
In this wonderful world she does no wrong
Charming all with her love that last so long
Here she must still learn to stand very strong
Every thought that she has focus on love
Look how she soars like a plane high above
Look how she is patient she does not shove
Ever she spreads her wings just like a dove

Mighty she has a magnificent mind
In this wonderful world she is so kind
Calling to her friends her sweet voice will bind
Here in this sweet song she's a perfect find
Excellently she shines bright in the night
Living lovingly with Friends she don't fight
Look how she creates beauty for the sight
Each day here she fights to do what is right

Monica

Making sure to shine bright every day
Opening a world ready for romance
Nothing will stop her in her work or play
In this wonderful world she loves to dance
Carefully she calls and she'll lead the way
Always she will give love in life a chance

Making sure to smile with eyes like a light
Opening her mighty mind to teach all
No one can deny that this star shines bright
In this world she takes time and will not fall
Charming she is such a wonderful sight
Always she listens for her true loves call

Making herself move as she sings her rhyme
Opening her loving heart to the Friend
No one here can accuse her of a crime
In this wonderful world she don't pretend
Carefully she thinks thoughts through out all time
Always a superstar until the END

Myisha

Mystifying men with her lovely smile
Yes her cheer and charm brightens the dark days
In this world she is a Queen whit such style
Shining awesomely she stands strong always
Having the heart to run the hardest mile
Always she will work as hard as she plays

Making Life more interesting in Time
Yes she lives lie a bird how she flies free
In this world she is a radiant Rhyme
She sets the standard for others to see
Here she will never commit any crime
Always an awesome Angel she will be

Many will find her a true Friend to Find
Yes she lives singing her song so well
It is her music's magic that will bind
She will spread the light where ever she dwell
Having a humble heart and staying kind
Always she will strive to stay out of hell!!!

Nafisa

Nature's beauty wrapped in beautiful skin
An awesome queen like those of ancient times
Fighting for what is right we know she'll win
Inspirer of invincible rhymes
She shines like the sun and behaves like kin
Always adorable in all the lines

Naturally attracting men with her mind
All the wise women see her as a queen
Friendly and caring she is a great find
In this special story she move the scene
Saving her favored friends when in a bind
Always a lasting friend on who to lean

Nurturing and gentile's her humble heart
Always accepting only what is best
Free like a bird is how she plays her part
In this world she will triumph through life's test
Shining awesomely she's a work of art
Always to be honored from east to west

<u>Naresh</u>

Nice as they come this caring gentle star
Always he shows such a kind human heart
Read like a bird he will fly so far
Each day he takes time to do his good part
Stopping to learn from his friends who they are
He stands with a sweet smile a work of art

No one can say his smile does not shine bright
Always in his voice you hear words so kind
Ready to live with love and share his light
Each friend that meets him knows he's a great find
Swiftly he will not do what is right
He has a great heart and a mighty mind

Needless to say he will shine in this Rhyme
Always his enchanting eyes will not bend
Ready to serve Lord Krsna through all time
Each person he meets knows he don't pretend
Sharing good deeds he does not commit crime
He soars like an eagle until time Ends

Natalie

Never was there such a sweet precious smile
Always a happy heart when I see her
Taking her time she moves with such sweet style
Always she is kind just like a sister
Love for you I'll travel more than a mile
In this world we will withstand the weather
Each moment pure pleasure none that is vile

No one can question her goodness of heart
Always she stands strong with beautiful eyes
The vibrant voice she has will sing her part
Always she will shine under God great skies
Like the great painter her heart is pure art
In her there is only truth and not lies
Each day she's up with love right from the start

Now is the time for her to share her mind
Always enchanting each one that she meets
This Lion Lady is gentle and kind
Always she is sweet to those that she greets
Letting the Buddha spirit be the bind
In this world she is the sweetest of treats
Everyone thinks that she is a great find

Nicholas

No one can defeat his true devotion
It is he who will work with great action
Careful and calm in his presentation
His heart live in goodness not in passion
Opening his heart he's a champion
Like the Lion he gives great protection
Always he chooses to give compassion
Sharing his style making a new fashion

Now he stands strong a great friend one may find
In this cryptic world he still remains kind
Calling with chants to friends that he will bind
He's really cool and know how to us wind
Orating wisdom's words from his great mind
Like the leader he leaves no one behind
Always awesome he is never unkind
Saintly in his ways wrong doers he'll grind

Nickey

No One except Her can sing Her song right
In this wonderful world She is so kind
Caring to love others and show them light
Keeping Her Friends happy She is a Find
Ever a sweet shining star she is bright
Yes She also has a real mighty mind

No One can tell me that Her Loves not real
I have seen her glorious form flow free
Causing this human heart to start to feel
Kind and so sweet is she when she sees me
Ever a true Friend for years that's the deal
Yes She is so beautiful as far as I see

No One should trouble this pretty princess
In this wonderful world She is a Friend
Caring to stop Strife and ease all distress
Keeping it real She knows not to pretend
Each one that sees Her should see happiness
Yes, She is enchanting until the End.

__Omar__

Opening his mind and heart to a friend
Many will see how he shines like a star
Always he is real right until the end
Ready to travel many miles so far

Opening his great gentle soul to all
Many will see him shine strong like the sun
Always he will answer a good friend's call
Ready to assist all 'till time is done

Opening his mouth with words that's so kind
Many will want to be near him always
Always he will be a great Friend to find
Readily he provides Hope all his days

Opening his great generous soul here
Many will want to get to know his name
Always he will live life with love not fear
Ready to be strong and go find his fame

Patty

Peaceful she shines like the sun in sky
Attracting all this Lady is Divine
This lovely Lady makes men's soul soar high
Radiantly she moves she is so fine
In her world is wisdom that is no lie
Charming is she peace and love is her sign.
In this world very high Patty will fly
Always so gentle she's sweet and sublime

Pleasant she is so thoughtful and kind
Attracting the best in life through out of time
This tough young lady's a true star I find
Readily she shares in life her sweet rhyme
In life a precious princess in my mind
Careful in life not to commit a crime
In life she shines bright don't leave her behind
An awesome being she's until life's last chime.

Rahul

Radiating like the sun in the sky
Always he will stand strong and sing his song
He is a falcon in the sky so high
Up from dawn until dusk he will stand strong
Living with the truth his heart does not lie

Ready to open his mystical mind
Always he will share with a friend some time
He is a pure friend a true precious find
Making his mark while he lives his life's rhyme
Like the great king he is thoughtful and kind

Ready like a lion this man will roar
Always with open eyes to see the real
He will fly free here just watch how he'll soar
Under God's great sky he'll tell you the deal
Look he's exciting he's not a bore

Ready is this powerful prince to rule
Always he will remain a favored friend
He will show the world that he is no fool
Uplifting others until the world end
Like a shining star this man is so cool.

<u>Raj</u>

Ready to shine like a star he is kind
A wise and wonderful person to meet
Just in his actions he is a rare find

Ready to defend and he can't be beat
A true devotee with a mighty mind
Just see ho easy he'll make a great feat

Ready to teach the world what's truly right
Always living life with good intention
Just a champion for friends he will fight

Ready to provide the strong protection
A man that give the world satisfaction
Just in his thought and kind in his action

Ready to take charge he will lead the way
All who follow him surely will shine
Just a pleasant person every day

Ready to write in life his perfect Rhyme
Always peaceful and kind at work or play
Just a thoughtful being through out all time

<u>Roberta</u>

Readily she shines sweetly with pure love
Opening her wonderful heart to all
Brilliantly she soars just like a dove
Each one she meets she respects big or small
Radiant she shines like the sun above
Taking care of all souls short or tall
Always she has a smile for The Belove

Readily she takes the time to be kind
Opening her mighty mind to the Friend
Bringing joy to each life that she will find
Each one knows she's real, she does not pretend
Ready with kind words to help you unwind
The shining star will shine until the end
Always with truthful words her actions bind

Readily she walks with Love here through time
Opening her soul she will lead the way
Bringing the best that she can to life's rhyme
Each one will want to hear what she will say
Repudiate any one who commits crime
This shining star surely brightens each day
Always she is sweet not sour like lime

<u>Romano</u>

Radiant is his gentle sunshine smile
Openly he shows he cares for his friends
Making goodness his great and grand style
All will appreciate the Love that he sends
No one will find bad things on this man's file
Openly he sets only the good trends

Readily he displays his devotion
Open are his calm blue enchanting eyes
Man among men he makes awesome action
Always so truthful he does not tell lies
No one can check his mystical motion
Openly he comforts that soul who cries

Readily his Love sins of the supreme
Openly he will show this world he's kind
Many will think that this man is a dream
Always he will be a friend's favorite find
Needless to say he is part of the team
Openly he shares his kind loving mind.

Rosa

Ready to take care of all she is sweet
Opening her loving heart to the friend
Seeing her shine in this world is a treat
Always she's sincere she does not pretend

Ready to speak for what she knows is right
Opening her mighty mind with great care
She lives in pure peace she's not here to fight
Always she will stand strong without the fear

Ready with courage to win in this life
Opening he sweet soul she sings her songs
Showing compassion she helps stop life's strife
Always she will do what's right not what's wrong

Ready to live life's sweet rhythm and beat
Opening her door for friends she defend
Shining like a priestess she does not cheat
Always an excellent friend tills the end

Saera

She shines a brilliant beam of light
Always wishing all other happiness
Ever shining like a star she is bright
Ready to bring the light through the darkness
Always aspiring to do what's right

She sings her sweet song and dances through time
Always she will enchant all with her voice
Each day she lives life with Love in this Rhyme
Ready to dispel darkness and rejoice
Always she will share her best loving line

She opens her mighty mind and her heart
Always she will like a lion shine bold
Each day she will want to play her great part
Ready to care for others she's not cold
Always she lives life a true work of art

She stands strong here to protect the true Friend
Always she will strive to fulfill the need
Each action always real she don't pretend
Ready to Help she is swift like a steed
Always she will shine right until the END.

Samuel

Shining so bright he is the Super Star
Always assisting Brothers when they call
Master among men he will travel far
Under the Great God's sky he will not fall
Ever he will remember who we are
Living life with power he does not stall

Showing the steps to the men in the dark
Awesome like a stone statue is His will
Making sure to share knowledge he's the spark
Under the sweet sun shine he won't stand still
Each day moving mightily he won't park
Living life with Love he don't want to kill

Sharing he great soul with those that he trust
An awesome person and a caring Friend
Making sure that what we do will be just
Under the night time sky Friends he defend
Ever living life with Love and not lust
Looking out for favored friends 'till the End

Sayra

Sweetly she smiles as she sings her good lines
Always an awesome person to talk to
Yes she radiates as she sing her rhymes
Readily for her friends she will come through
A true bright star that shines through the bad times

She has such strong focus enchanting eyes
Always open to observe the real dead
Yes like the sun she brightens up the skies
Readily she will tell all what is real
Always awesome she'll have you mesmerized

Showing the whole world her beauty each day
Always her pleasant thoughts are attractive
Yes she will take a stand and lead the way
Readily it's her goodness she will give
Always she has something that's sweet to say

Sharing her good heart with all of her friends
Always she will overcome this life's test
Yes she is truthful and she sets the trends
Readily she makes friends from east to west
A true champion 'till this world ends

Shamora

She is a great goddess gentle and kind
Here her sweet smile will brighten the day
Always she speaks thoughtful thoughts from her mind
Many will find she shines like the sun's Ray
Openly she tells the truth you will find
Ready is lioness to lead the sway
An awesome friend to help the mind unwind

She is stable like a tree in this life
Here she has a good nature for us all
Always she will surely survive life's strife
Making sure that favored friends will not fall
Only living in love not with the knife
Readily she takes time to climb the wall
As for her future a wonderful wife

She is consistent and full of great care
Here she shines bright like a true super star
Always she's calm with courage not fear
Many of her friends she will help more far
On time is she to lend her friend an ear
Ready to live life peace and not wear
Always great loving heart Shamora will share

Sivakami

She is a thoughtful terrific person
Inside her heart lives such a kind princess
Victoriously she'll learn life's lesson
Always she will help to destroy distress
Kind like the sun her smile will shine on all
Always her deep dark brown eyes are peaceful
Many will find her a good friend to call
It is her bright soul that keeps her blissful

She will stand strong and sing her sweet love song
In her humble heart she will do what's right
Valiantly she will correct what's wrong
Always she'll display her minds mighty might
Keeping her goodness a Lovely Lady
A rose among flowers she is so sweet
Many will see and angel she will be
It is her presence that is such a treat

<u>Sweetie</u>

Singing her song with her sweet gentle voice
Waking the world up to live in true love
Each one that hears here will want to rejoice
Every song will help her rise above
This wonderful woman is a great choice
In this wonderful world she's like the dove

Smiling brightly with her endearing eyes
Walking through the world a true great Goddess
Each time that she shines she'll brighten the skies
Each time that she speaks creates happiness
This wonderful woman does not tell lies
In this sweet story she's here for greatness
Each day she triumphs you will realize

Shining like a jewel her heart is so kind
Women adore her and men give her praise
Each one that meets here will see she's a great find
Each one that meets her their spirit she'll raise
This lovely lady is a friend to bind
In this wonderful world she'll shine all days
Each one that meets her will Love her great mind

Tammy

Taking her time she takes care of the friend
An Awesome woman whose light will shine bright
Make sure and know she's real she don't pretend
Many will be blessed by her lovely light
Yes she will be a true friend in the end

This shining star will live like as a dance
Always traveling a true champion
Many will be blessed just by her great glance
Many will find she's always in fashion
Yes in her heart she seeks the true romance

Taking her sweet time she will see her dream
Always loving in this world she is kind
Many will want to be part of her team
Many will see she's a wonderful find
Yes she will shine here just like a true queen

Taking her time with true friends she will share
Always listening and speaking a love
Magnificently she shows she will care
Making her mark here she will rise above
Yes she will live in a love and not fear

<u>Tony</u>

Thoughtful is he who truly takes his time
Opening the mind to give others care
Now he radiantly will live his rhyme
Yes, he will live life with courage not fear

This being is brilliant gentle and kind
Openly he will make this world better
Now he is a favored friend and great find
Yes, he keeps his word right to the letter

Triumphantly he will move through this life
Openly he will shine a big bright star
Now in this life he will help to stop strife
Yes he will live free and will travel far

The Doctor ho not only saves the spine
One man who helps his patients rise above
Now he will live life and leave the great line
Yes he is sure to show them care and love

Tsering

This wonderful woman wants to be free
She shines like the high star deep in the dark
Ever she is calm like a tranquil sea
Ready to stand strong like trees in a park
I is her super strength that this world will see
Now she has sweet words to say so please hark
Given the time she will sing perfectly

This lovely lady has a tender heart
She puts together great things in the play
Ever she will shine brightly right from the start
Ready to dispense the darkness each day
In this awesome world she's a work of art
Now she will take the lead and lead the way
Giving gentle thoughts not thoughts that are tart

This lovely lady is such a kind friend
She stays in touch with a beautiful bind
Ever her goodness through time she will send
Ready to be real friend you will find
In this wonderful world she don't pretend
Now see how she is so careful and kind
Giving her true love to friends 'till the end

<u>Van</u>

Very bright and beautiful is this Queen
Always she will shine like a super star
No one can deny she's pure and pristine

Very lovely in life she will go far
Always she adds life and love to the scene
Now she promotes pure peace and not war

Very enchanting her lovely eyes shine
Always thoughtful is lady's mighty mind
No one can say that she is not Devine

Very friendly like kind she is so kind
Always her sweet lips has a loving line
Now know that she is a true special find

Very harmonious is her hearts song,
Always she will sing as she shines her light
No one will stop her for her heart is strong

Very caring and sharing she shines bright
Always her pure poetry will be strong
Now watch her fly like an eagle in flight.

__Victor__

Victorious is this man in this time
It is his sunshine smile that gives us light
Carefully caring for all in Life's Rhyme
This pure person here does not want to fight
Openly chastising those who do crime
Readily is he to do what is right

Victorious comes mighty man each day
It is his humble heart that sing The song
Carefully thinking about what he'll say
This man like a tree can stand all day long
Opening his mind to friends in this play
Readily he calmly corrects the wrong

Victoriously is how he lives life
In this man lives a mighty mystic now
Carefully creating a block to Strife
This man has walked so many miles some how
Openly he lives with Love not the knife
Readily he sings until time to bow!!!

<u>Vidya</u>

Valiant she roars like a great Lioness
It is her good heart that will lead the way
Doing her best is this pretty princess
You will love the wonderful words she say
Always there to help those in great distress

Virtuous is this shining loving star
In this day and time she chants the great name
Doing her best in life she will go far
You will see how she gains eternal fame
Always she takes time and learns who we are

Very impressive is this champion
It is she who will stand and take the lead
Doing her best with her words of action
You will see she'll deliver a great deed
Always friendly she shows such great fashion

Vibrant her light shines bright in the world here
It is her mighty mind that makes her great
Doing her best she lives life without fear
You will see how she conquers you just wait
Always for true friends she show that she care

Viryavan

Very strong this star will shine all day long
In this world he will share his awesome art
Radiating lyrics of love in song
You see he shine right from the very start
Always he does what is right not what's wrong
Valiantly he will play his great part
As his name states he will always stand strong
No one will ever discourage his heart.

Victorious he will be kind king
In this world he serves Krsna throughout time
Ready to call us to chant or to sing
You will see he tries not to commit crime
Always a beautiful mind he will bring
Virtuous he is the star of this rhyme
As always he seeks to do the right thing
Now in this world he will shine through out time

Walter

Wonderfully enchanting are his way
A mighty man whose light will always shine
Lifting up others on their darkest days
Taking the time to show us were divine
Enhancing other lives with loving rays
Readily he sends you a saving line

Willing to assist all Friends big or small
Allowing all to share in his great light
Looking out for Friends as that they won't fall
Touching other lives with outstanding might
Ever a proud protector in the All
Readily he will do what's truly right

Waking up each day with a heart so kind
Although gentle he still stands very tough
Letting all know he has a mighty mind
That man's like a stone solid rough
Each one that meets him with goodness he'll bind
Ready to tell others that is enough

<u>Will</u>

Wonderfully he works to make this world grand
It is his will hat will make him shine bright
Leading like a lion he takes a stand
Letting his conscious tell him what is right

With strength and courage he will forge his path
IN this wonderful world he is a star
Living in perfect order like good math
Living like an eagle he will soar far

Walking with zeal and a wonderful mind
It is his will to see this world improve
Like a good father he is happy and kind
Like a great dancer he stays in the groove

What a radiant representative
It is he who will shine every day
Like an angel he has so much to give
Look how he will shine in every way.

<u>Winnie</u>

Wonderful is this world's Precious Princess
In her is the heart and key to heaven
No one can challenge her or cause her stress
No one can steal her great sacred seven
It is her smile that shines through her best dress
Each man sees she's a jewel among women

Wonderful is this sweet Lovely Lady
In this world she will fly high like a dove
Never will her love stop flowing like the sea
Never in time, this world she will not love
In this world a great goddess she will be
Each day she will soar and shine high above

Wonderful an awesome Asian Angel
It is her enchanting eyes that shine bright
Needless to say that she wishes all well
No one will ever block out Lady's Light
It is destiny she'll shine where she dwell
Each day she'll defend her minds great might

Yesenia

Yes she is so sweet with a mighty mind
Enchanting are her bright eyes and her smile
She shines a warm gentle star who is kind
Each one that meets her loves her special style
No one can say she is not a special find
In time for her I go the extra mile
An awesome find that will help you unwind

Yes she stands a sweet beautiful lady
Each smile that she gives will brighten the day
See how her love surrounds you like the sea
Each one marvels at her mystical way
No one can say that she's not poetry
In my world for her happiness I pray
Always a sweet soul in her there will be

Yes in this great life she will stand strong
Each one that meets her sees she is the best
She sings her sweet song with friends all day long
Enchanting lady shines from east to west
Needless to say she does what's right not wrong
In her wonderful heart in her chest
Always she will share her loving song